Awakened Living: Embrace Mindfulness for a Fulfilling Life

I. Introduction

A. Overview of Mindfulness
1. Defining Mindfulness: Beyond Meditation
2. Historical Roots and Evolution
3. Modern Relevance and Applications

B. The Importance of Awakened Living
1. Connecting Mindfulness to a Fulfilling Life
2. Addressing the Need for Conscious Awareness
3. Setting Expectations for the Journey Ahead

C. Setting the Tone for a Fulfilling Life
1. Establishing the Mind-Body Connection
2. The Role of Mindfulness in Well-being
3. Inviting the Reader to Embrace Change

II. The Power of Mindfulness

A. Exploring the Essence of Mindfulness
1. Delving into Present-Moment Awareness
2. Understanding Non-Judgmental Observation
3. Embracing Mindfulness as a State of Being

B. Scientific Basis and Benefits
1. Neuroscience of Mindfulness
2. Psychological and Emotional Impacts
3. Mindfulness and Physical Health

C. Mindfulness vs. Mindlessness
1. Contrasting Mindful and Automatic Living
2. Recognizing Signs of Mindlessness
3. The Transformative Power of Mindful Living

III. Cultivating Presence in Daily Life

A. Mindful Awareness in Everyday Activities
1. Infusing Mindfulness into Routine Tasks
2. The Beauty of Simple Moments
3. Breaking Free from Multitasking

B. Breaking the Cycle of Autopilot
1. Uncovering Habits and Patterns
2. Mindful Interruptions to Automatic Responses
3. The Liberating Nature of Conscious Choices

C. Creating Space for Presence
1. The Art of Mindful Pause
2. Mindfulness in Chaos
3. Building Mental Resilience through Presence

IV. Mindful Breathing: A Gateway to Awareness

A. Understanding the Breath-Mind Connection
1. Breath as an Anchor to the Present
2. Mindful Breathing Techniques
3. Integrating Breath Awareness into Daily Life

B. Techniques for Mindful Breathing
1. Diaphragmatic Breathing
2. Box Breathing and Variations
3. Mindful Breathing for Stress Reduction

C. Integrating Breath Awareness into Daily Routines
1. Mindful Breathing at Work
2. Mindful Breathing in Relationships
3. Sustaining Breath Awareness Beyond Formal Practice.

V. Embracing the Present Moment

A. The Art of Being Present
1. Presence in Conversation and Connection
2. Mindful Observation of Nature and Surroundings

3. Present-Moment Joy and Contentment

B. Letting Go of Past Regrets and Future Worries
1. Mindful Release of Regret and Guilt
2. Overcoming Anxiety About the Future
3. The Freedom of Now

C. Finding Joy in the Now
1. Cultivating Gratitude
2. Mindful Pleasure and Enjoyment
3. Savoring Life's Simple Pleasures

VI. Nurturing Mindful Relationships

A. Mindful Communication
1. The Role of Listening in Communication
2. Expressing Yourself Mindfully
3. Resolving Conflicts with Presence

B. Building Empathy and Compassion
1. Understanding Empathy in Mindful Relationships
2. Compassion as a Natural Outcome of Mindfulness
3. Extending Kindness to Others and Yourself

C. Strengthening Connections Through Presence
1. Quality Time and Mindful Presence
2. Shared Mindfulness Practices
3. The Ripple Effect of Mindful Relationships

VII. Mindful Practices for Inner Peace

A. Meditation and Mindfulness Exercises
1. Exploring Various Meditation Techniques
2. Mindfulness in Movement: Yoga and Walking
3. Developing a Personal Meditation Routine

B. Creating a Personal Mindfulness Routine
1. Designing a Daily Mindfulness Schedule

2. Integrating Mindfulness into Work and Leisure
3. Overcoming Challenges in Establishing a Routine

C. Harnessing Inner Peace Amidst Chaos
1. Mindfulness in Stressful Situations
2. Finding Calm in the Midst of Turbulence
3. The Transformative Power of Inner Peace

VIII. Mindful Decision-Making and Action

A. Applying Mindfulness to Choices
1. Mindful Decision-Making Principles
2. The Art of Deliberation
3. The Consequences of Mindful Choices

B. Intentional Action and Consequence
1. Aligning Actions with Values
2. Mindful Execution of Tasks and Goals
3. Learning from Consequences with Compassion

C. Mindful Leadership and Responsibility
1. Mindfulness in Leadership Roles
2. Navigating Ethical Dilemmas with Mindfulness
3. Inspiring Others through Mindful Leadership

IX. Overcoming Challenges with Mindfulness

A. Mindfulness as a Coping Mechanism
1. Coping with Stress and Anxiety
2. Mindfulness in Times of Grief and Loss
3. Building Emotional Resilience

B. Resilience in the Face of Adversity
1. Embracing Impermanence and Change
2. The Role of Mindfulness in Adapting to Challenges
3. Transforming Pain into Growth

C. Transforming Challenges into Growth Opportunities
1. The Mindful Perspective on Challenges

2. Finding Meaning and Purpose in Difficulties
3. Resilience and Growth Through Mindfulness

X. Sustaining a Fulfilling Life: Mindfulness in the Long Run

A. Making Mindfulness a Lifelong Practice
1. The Evolution of Mindfulness Practices
2. Staying Inspired on the Mindfulness Journey
3. Integrating Mindfulness Across the Lifespan

B. Mindful Goal Setting and Achievement
1. Setting Intentional and Mindful Goals
2. The Role of Patience and Persistence
3. Celebrating Success Mindfully

C. Reflections on a Fulfilling and Awakened Life
1. Reflecting on Personal Growth and Transformation
2. Gratitude and Mindfulness
3. Inspiring Others to Embark on the Path of Awakened Living

Introduction

Welcome to a transformative journey through the heartbeat of urban life—a journey that transcends the skyscrapers, the hustle, and the relentless pace of the city. In the pages that follow, you are invited to step into a world where mindfulness becomes a guiding light, weaving seamlessly through the fabric of everyday existence. This is "Awakened Living: Embrace Mindfulness for a Fulfilling Life."

In a city where dreams are as vast as the skyline, and ambitions resonate in every echoing footstep, mindfulness takes center stage in reshaping how we perceive and experience the world.

Embark on a Unique Adventure:

This isn't just a book; it's a roadmap to a life rich with awareness, meaning, and fulfillment. Join me as we navigate the bustling streets, engage with diverse communities, and uncover the transformative power of mindfulness in every corner of urban life.

A Symphony of Chapters:

Our journey begins with the essence of mindful awareness, where the city's chaotic rhythm becomes the backdrop for discovering the beauty in simplicity. Together, we'll explore the intricate dance between mind and body, dive into self-awareness, and breathe in the present moment amidst the urban cacophony.

As we traverse the cityscape, relationships become a canvas, and resilience emerges as a response to life's inevitable challenges. We'll navigate the crossroads of decision-making, embrace inner peace amidst chaos, and find solace in mindfulness practices that extend far beyond the city limits.

A Lifelong Exploration:

Join me in uncovering the evolving nature of mindfulness—a practice not confined to meditation cushions but intricately woven into the ever-changing circumstances of our lives. As we delve into advanced techniques and mindfulness retreats, consider the profound connection between mindfulness and spiritual development.

Balancing mindfulness with ambition, navigating relationships across a lifetime, and leaving behind a legacy of awakened living—these are the chapters that complete our narrative. Each page invites you to explore, reflect, and integrate mindfulness into your own life, whether you're amidst the city lights or in the serenity of your own space.

Your Invitation to Awakened Living:

So, are you ready to embark on this journey? Turn the page, dive into the chapters, and let the city's energy infuse your exploration of mindfulness. Allow the rhythm of New York to harmonize with the profound teachings of awareness, presence, and intentional living.

Awakened Living is not just a destination; it's a lifelong journey—one that starts with the turn of the first page. Let the adventure begin and may the exploration of mindfulness enrich every step of your unique urban odyssey.

Chapter One: The Profound Tapestry of Mindfulness

A. Defining Mindfulness: Beyond Meditation

In the intricate tapestry of our modern lives, mindfulness emerges as a golden thread, delicately weaving its way through the cacophony of our thoughts and emotions. Its essence extends far beyond the oft-associated images of meditation and yoga; instead, it unfolds as a profound way of being—a dance of intentional and non-judgmental awareness in the present moment. This chapter embarks on a captivating odyssey, inviting readers to delve into the very soul of mindfulness and its intricate influence on the fabric of our daily existence.

1.1 The Essence of Mindfulness: A Symphony of Awareness

Mindfulness is the art of paying attention—an intentional cultivation of awareness, a deliberate choice to engage fully with the symphony of thoughts, emotions, and surroundings that compose the present moment. In the depth of mindfulness, we find not an escape from reality but an immersive embrace, an invitation to encounter life with heightened consciousness. This section beckons readers into a reflective journey, urging them to explore the nuanced dance of intentional living through the lens of mindfulness.

1.2 Historical Roots and Evolution: A Timeless Journey

To unravel the profound tapestry of mindfulness, we journey back through the corridors of time, tracing its historical roots deeply embedded in ancient contemplative practices. From the fertile grounds of Buddhist traditions to the diverse landscapes of contemplative practices across cultures, mindfulness emerges as a timeless wisdom that has traversed centuries. Understanding its historical context becomes the key to unlocking its relevance—a relevance that transcends cultural boundaries, resonating as a universal guide for the contemporary seeker.

1.3 Modern Relevance and Applications: A Cultural Metamorphosis

In the labyrinth of today's fast-paced world, mindfulness evolves beyond its traditional spiritual and cultural contexts. This exploration unfolds the modern relevance of mindfulness, showcasing its applications as far-reaching threads woven into the fabric of diverse fields. From mental health and education to the corporate landscape, mindfulness becomes more than a personal practice—it metamorphoses into a societal shift, a collective movement towards greater presence, well-being, and interconnectedness.

B. Scientific Basis and Benefits

Mindfulness, often painted as a subjective experience, finds validation in the crucible of science. Its transformative effects on the brain and overall well-being are not mere metaphors but concrete realities substantiated by rigorous scientific inquiry.

1.1 Neuroscience of Mindfulness: Orchestrating Brain Harmony

Venturing into the intricate landscapes of neuroscience, we unravel the symphony behind mindfulness. This exploration navigates the fascinating realm where regular mindfulness practice becomes a maestro, reshaping the brain's structure and function through the dance of neuroplasticity. As we traverse the neural pathways, readers gain a deeper understanding of the tangible effects of mindfulness, witnessing the intricate harmony it orchestrates within the brain.

1.2 Psychological and Emotional Impacts: Nurturing the Garden of the Mind

The psychological benefits of mindfulness are an expansive garden, bearing fruits of stress reduction, enhanced emotional regulation, and the nurturing of mental resilience. Through research-backed insights, readers embark on a profound journey into the psychological and emotional landscapes cultivated by mindfulness. It becomes a sanctuary, a refuge for the mind to flourish and navigate the intricacies of the human experience with grace and wisdom.

1.3 Mindfulness and Physical Health: The Holistic Symphony

Expanding beyond the confines of the mind, mindfulness extends its benevolent touch to physical well-being. This section embarks on a journey through studies showcasing the impact of mindfulness on immune function, cardiovascular health, and overall longevity. The intricate dance between mind and body becomes an art, a holistic symphony where mindfulness practices compose the notes that resonate through the entire being.

C. Mindfulness vs. Mindlessness

To fully appreciate the spectrum of mindfulness, we plunge into its counterpart—mindlessness. By illuminating the stark differences between these two states of being, we unveil the subtle ways in which mindlessness infiltrates our lives, often robbing us of the richness inherent in our experiences.

1.1 Contrasting Mindful and Automatic Living: The Unseen Ballet

Mindlessness often masquerades as the default mode—a ballet of automatic living characterized by habitual reactions and a lack of conscious presence. Through poignant real-life examples and narratives, we vividly contrast mindless and mindful living. Readers are invited to witness the unseen ballet, recognizing the moments when they might be operating on autopilot, disconnected from the vibrant tapestry of life.

1.2 Recognizing Signs of Mindlessness: Illuminating the Shadows

Identification is the first step towards transformation. This section becomes a lantern, illuminating the shadows where signs of mindlessness often lurk. From the subtle cues embedded in daily routines to the more profound moments of autopilot living, readers gain awareness of when they might be operating without conscious intent. Through this recognition, a pathway to breaking free from the cycle of unconscious living begins to unfold.

1.3 The Transformative Power of Mindful Living: An Awakening

As the chapter gracefully concludes, we transcend the notion of mindfulness as a mere practice. It emerges as a shift in perspective—an awakening—a conscious choice to savor the richness of each moment. The transformative power of mindfulness isn't confined to a meditation cushion; it permeates every fiber of our existence. The journey into mindfulness is not just a practice; it is an awakening—an invitation to live with intention, presence, and the promise of a profoundly fulfilled life.

In the following pages, we delve even deeper, exploring the intricate nuances of mindfulness, its applications in various facets of life, and the art of integrating mindfulness into the tapestry of our everyday existence. The journey continues, promising revelations and a deeper understanding of the art of awakened living.

Chapter Two: The Transformative Tapestry of Mindfulness

A. Exploring the Essence of Mindfulness

2.1 Delving into Present-Moment Awareness: A Symphony of Now

In the boundless universe of mindfulness, the exploration of present-moment awareness becomes a journey into the very heart of existence. This section invites readers to not merely dip their toes but to plunge into the ocean of the present—a boundless sea where past regrets and future anxieties dissolve. Through guided exercises that awaken the senses, readers embark on a sensorial odyssey, immersing themselves in the richness of each moment. The art of present-moment awareness is unveiled as more than a technique; it is a profound connection to the eternal now—a gateway to experiencing the fullness of life.

2.2 Understanding Non-Judgmental Observation: The Compassionate Gaze

In the expansive landscape of mindfulness, the art of non-judgmental observation emerges as a gentle yet powerful force—a compassionate gaze that transcends the dualities of right and wrong. Building on the foundation of Chapter One, this section delves deeper into the transformative power of non-judgment. Through experiential exercises rooted in self-compassion, readers are guided to dismantle the walls of self-criticism. The compassionate gaze becomes a mirror reflecting not only the nuances of the internal landscape but also the inherent dignity and worthiness of every thought and emotion—a pathway to profound self-acceptance.

2.3 Embracing Mindfulness as a State of Being: Living Artfully

Beyond a compendium of practices, mindfulness is an artful way of living—an ongoing masterpiece that transcends the constraints of routine. This section peels back the layers, inviting readers to view mindfulness not as a periodic retreat but as an integral aspect of daily life. By exploring the integration of mindfulness into routine moments, readers discover that every mundane act, from sipping tea to commuting, can be a canvas for mindful living. The chapter concludes with a realization—an awakening to mindfulness as a transformative force, seamlessly woven into the fabric of every breath, every step, and every heartbeat.

B. Scientific Basis and Benefits

2.1 Neuroscience of Mindfulness: Illuminating Neural Pathways

The journey into the neuroscience of mindfulness becomes an intricate tapestry of neurons, synapses, and profound transformations. Building on the foundational understanding from Chapter One, this section ventures even deeper into the neural symphony orchestrated by mindfulness. Through the lens of scientific studies, readers gain an intimate understanding of how mindfulness literally reshapes the neural pathways associated with attention, emotional regulation, and self-awareness. The narrative becomes a guided tour through the neural landscapes, illuminating the tangible changes within the brain's architecture as it harmonizes with the practice of mindfulness.

2.2 Psychological and Emotional Impacts: The Healing Embrace

The psychological and emotional impacts of mindfulness become a therapeutic sanctuary—a space where the mind unfolds its wings and soars. Building on the therapeutic garden metaphor, this section explores the transformative potential of mindfulness in alleviating conditions such as anxiety, depression, and stress. Real-life stories become windows into the profound shifts in emotional well-being brought about by mindfulness. Practical exercises, now with a more immersive quality, invite readers to actively engage with mindfulness as a tool for emotional healing. The chapter becomes a refuge—a testament to the depth of emotional resilience that mindfulness can cultivate.

2.3 Mindfulness and Physical Health: The Dance of Wholeness

The exploration of the mind-body connection evolves into a dance—a choreography of wholeness where mindfulness becomes the guiding partner. This section immerses readers in the myriad ways mindfulness influences physical health, from immune system enhancement to the alleviation of chronic pain. Real-world examples and evidence-based tips provide readers with a roadmap to incorporate mindfulness into their daily routines for optimal well-being. The chapter becomes a celebration—a dance of wholeness where mindfulness moves in harmony with the body, fostering a sense of holistic well-being.

C. Mindfulness vs. Mindlessness

2.1 Contrasting Mindful and Automatic Living: A Choreography of Consciousness

Building upon the exploration of mindlessness in Chapter One, the contrasts between mindful and automatic living deepen. Through evocative examples and relatable scenarios, readers are invited into a choreography of consciousness—a dance where each step is intentional. The narrative becomes a kaleidoscope, revealing the subtle ballet of mindful awareness amidst the cacophony of automatic habits. Readers are prompted to reflect not just on the consequences of mindless routines but on the untapped potential for transformation through intentional presence.

2.2 Recognizing Signs of Mindlessness: Unveiling the Subtle Shadows

The exploration of mindlessness becomes a journey into the shadows—unveiling the subtle cues that often go unnoticed. Through a comprehensive examination of everyday scenarios, readers deepen their self-awareness, becoming adept at recognizing the moments when they slip into autopilot. The goal transcends mere recognition; it becomes a call to action—an invitation to reclaim agency and redirect attention to the present. The chapter becomes a lantern, guiding readers through the shadows of mindlessness, fostering a sense of conscious participation in the unfolding narrative of their lives.

2.3 The Transformative Power of Mindful Living: A Symphony of Change

As the chapter gracefully concludes, the transformative power of mindful living echoes like a symphony—a harmonious interplay of intentional choices and awakened presence. Readers are prompted to reflect on the symphony of change that mindfulness can bring into their lives. The journey into mindfulness becomes not just a practice but a profound awakening—an invitation to live with intention, presence, and the promise of a profoundly fulfilled life.

In the following pages, we embark on an even more profound exploration, unraveling the complexities of mindfulness in various facets of life and uncovering the art of seamlessly integrating mindfulness into the intricate tapestry of our everyday existence.

Chapter Three: Cultivating Presence in Daily Life

A. Mindful Awareness in Everyday Activities

3.1 Infusing Mindfulness into Routine Tasks: A Symphony of Presence

In the vast landscape of mindfulness, the integration of mindfulness into routine tasks is not a mere suggestion; it is an art—a symphony of presence that beckons individuals to explore the profound depths within the ordinary. Let's take a plunge into the essence of infusing mindfulness into the mundane, transcending the notion that it's confined to meditation cushions. As we embark on this exploration, envision washing dishes not as a chore but as a tactile dance with the present moment, each movement an opportunity for profound awareness. Walking transforms from a means of reaching a destination to a rhythmic communion with the environment. Even the act of commuting, often seen as a mundane necessity, becomes a journey through mindful observation. Through practical examples and experiential exercises, readers will not only understand but deeply feel the transformative potential of infusing mindfulness into their daily rituals. This section becomes a guidebook for the reader, unlocking the doors to a world where every task, no matter how routine, becomes an opportunity for a symphony of presence.

3.2 The Beauty of Simple Moments: Savoring Life's Tapestry

In a world captivated by the allure of complexity, the beauty of simple moments often eludes our attention. This section invites readers to embark on a journey of savoring, where the ordinary is celebrated, and the mundane becomes extraordinary. Imagine finding profound joy in the warmth of sunlight streaming through a window or the rhythmic patter of raindrops on a rooftop. Through evocative narratives and contemplative exercises, readers will be guided to recognize and savor these simple moments, unveiling the richness woven into the tapestry of everyday life. This isn't just about understanding; it's about feeling the texture of life's tapestry in its simplest, most unadorned form. The chapter unfolds as an immersive experience, prompting readers to become connoisseurs of life's subtlest nuances.

3.3 Breaking Free from Multitasking: The Myth Unveiled

Multitasking, often hailed as a symbol of efficiency, unravels as a myth with profound consequences. Let's delve deeper into the intricacies of divided attention, dissecting the cognitive cost of juggling multiple tasks simultaneously. Engaging narratives and cognitive insights will serve as a magnifying glass, revealing the subtle yet pervasive impacts of multitasking on the quality of attention and overall well-being. The section doesn't just stop at debunking the myth; it unfolds into an exploration of the liberating practice of single tasking. We'll navigate through the immersive experience of doing one thing at a time, elevating it from a productivity hack to a mindful engagement with the present moment. By the end of this exploration, readers will not only comprehend the pitfalls of multitasking but will have the tools to consciously choose single tasking, transforming routine activities into intentional rituals.

B. Breaking the Cycle of Autopilot

3.1 Uncovering Habits and Patterns: A Journey Within

Mindfulness, at its core, requires a courageous inward journey—a deep dive into the sea of habits and automatic reactions that shape our daily existence. This isn't a surface-level examination; it's a profound exploration that demands introspection and self-discovery. Readers will be guided through exercises and real-life stories, shining a light on patterns that often operate in the shadows of our awareness. This self-awareness becomes the bedrock upon which intentional actions are built—an essential step in breaking free from the invisible chains of autopilot. By the end of this section, readers won't just understand the concept of habits; they'll have a visceral understanding of their own habitual responses, paving the way for transformative change.

3.2 Mindful Interruptions to Automatic Responses: Reclaiming Agency

The narrative deepens as we explore practical techniques for interrupting automatic responses. Imagine this as the process of reclaiming agency—a journey from reactive living to a conscious, intentional engagement with each passing moment. Through a series of mindfulness exercises and reflections, readers will not only learn how to pause but also how to assess and respond deliberately. This isn't a theoretical understanding; it's a toolkit for real-time application. The art of interrupting autopilot isn't just a concept to grasp; it's a transformative practice that empowers individuals to navigate the twists and turns of life with mindfulness at the helm. By the conclusion of this section, readers won't just know about mindfulness; they'll be actively embodying it in the rhythm of their daily lives.

3.3 The Liberating Nature of Conscious Choices: Crafting an Intentional Life

Conscious choices emerge as the keystones of an awakened life. This isn't a passive understanding; it's an active engagement with the philosophy that each moment presents an opportunity for a conscious choice. Picture responding to a challenge not with knee-jerk reactions but with equanimity or choosing gratitude over frustration in the face of adversity. The section unfolds as a cascade of intentional choices, each contributing to the mosaic of a mindful life. This isn't just a theoretical exploration of mindfulness; it's a series of actionable steps that individuals can take in their daily lives. By the end of this section, readers will not only appreciate the power of conscious choices but will be equipped with the awareness and tools to make them consistently, crafting an intentional and purposeful existence.

C. Creating Space for Presence

3.1 The Art of Mindful Pause: An Oasis in the Chaos

In the relentless rhythm of modern life, the mindful pause becomes an artful tool for creating space amidst the chaos. This section is a deep dive into various techniques for incorporating short pauses into the day. Guided practices become more than exercises; they are moments of respite, allowing individuals to reconnect with the present moment. The mindful pause isn't just a theoretical concept; it's an experiential journey. Readers will not only learn about creating space for presence but will actively practice it, weaving moments of tranquility into the fabric of their bustling schedules. This isn't just about understanding the importance of pause; it's about living it.

3.2 Mindfulness in Chaos: Navigating the Storm

Chaos, an inevitable part of the human experience, unfolds as a canvas for mindfulness. Let's guide readers through strategies for maintaining awareness during challenging situations. Whether facing stress, conflict, or uncertainty, the principles of mindfulness become steadfast anchors. This section is more than a theoretical exploration of mindfulness in chaotic moments; it's a hands-on guide to actively applying mindfulness in the stormy seas of life. Readers will not only understand the potential for mindfulness in chaos but will actively navigate the storm with an unwavering sense of grace. The chaos becomes not a hindrance but an opportunity for mindfulness to shine.

3.3 Building Mental Resilience through Presence: An Inner Fortress

As the chapter crescendos, we explore how mental resilience is cultivated through the consistent practice of mindfulness. The ability to stay present in the face of adversity becomes a testament to emotional strength and adaptability. This isn't just a theoretical exploration of resilience; it's a practical guide to building mental fortitude. By the end of this section, readers won't just know about mental resilience; they'll be actively engaged in the process of cultivating it—a resilient inner fortress that stands strong amidst life's challenges. This isn't just a chapter on mental resilience; it's a transformative journey into building a robust and adaptable mind.

As the exploration of cultivating presence in daily life unfolds, readers are immersed in the richness of mindfulness—a journey that goes beyond concepts and techniques, inviting them to embrace a life infused with profound awareness and intentionality. The tapestry of mindfulness is woven into the very fabric of existence, offering a transformative lens through which to perceive and engage with the world. This extended chapter serves as a comprehensive guide, providing not just knowledge but a lived experience of cultivating mindfulness in every facet of daily life.

Chapter Four: Mindful Breathing: A Gateway to Awareness

A. Understanding the Breath-Mind Connection

4.1 Breath as an Anchor to the Present: The Profound Symphony of Breath and Awareness

In the intricate dance of mindfulness, the breath emerges as a symphony conductor, orchestrating our connection to the present moment. This section takes a deep dive into the profound union of breath and awareness, portraying the breath as a constant companion available at any moment. Through immersive mindful breathing exercises, readers are not just told but invited to experience the transformative potential inherent in this deceptively simple yet profoundly impactful practice. The breath becomes more than just a physiological process; it becomes a rhythmic gateway to heightened consciousness.

Breath, the fundamental rhythm of life, serves as the anchor to the present, a bridge between the internal world of thoughts and emotions and the external world of experiences. It invites individuals to explore the subtle nuances of each inhalation and exhalation, transforming an automatic bodily function into a conscious and intentional act. The breath, like a guiding star, leads individuals back to the present moment, fostering a sense of groundedness and tranquility.

4.2 Mindful Breathing Techniques: Crafting a Personal Breath Symphony

Building upon the foundational understanding of breath awareness, we embark on a journey through a myriad of mindful breathing techniques. It's not a one-size-fits-all approach; readers are encouraged to explore and discover methods that resonate with their unique preferences and needs. Practical guidance transforms theoretical knowledge into lived experiences, ensuring that readers can seamlessly integrate these techniques into the intricate tapestry of their daily lives. Breath, once an involuntary act, becomes a conscious and intentional dance with the present moment.

The exploration of mindful breathing techniques is akin to discovering a personal breath symphony, where each technique is a note contributing to the harmonious composition of awareness. From diaphragmatic breathing to rhythmic patterns, readers are invited to experiment with various techniques, finding resonance with the ones that synchronize with their internal rhythms. The breathful symphony becomes not just a skill to be acquired but a personalized expression of mindfulness.

4.3 Integrating Breath Awareness into Daily Life: The Breathful Art of Living

Breath awareness transcends the boundaries of formal meditation—it becomes a companion seamlessly woven into the fabric of daily activities. Readers are gently ushered into the concept of breath as a constant guide, navigating them through the ebb and flow of work, relationships, and moments of solitude. By the culmination of this chapter, individuals are not just informed but equipped with a toolkit for maintaining a steadfast connection to the present through the rhythmic dance of conscious breathing. Life becomes a breathful art, and every moment an opportunity for mindful living.

The integration of breath awareness into daily life is a transformative journey where the breath becomes an ever-present ally. From the moment of awakening in the morning to the act of sipping a cup of tea, readers learn to infuse each activity with the rhythm of conscious breathing. The breathful art of living extends beyond formal practices, becoming a way of being—a continuous dance with the present moment. Whether in the midst of a busy day at work or during moments of quiet reflection, individuals discover the subtle yet profound impact of breathful living.

B. Techniques for Mindful Breathing

4.1 Diaphragmatic Breathing: Nurturing the Breathful Roots

Deep diaphragmatic breathing takes center stage in this expansive section, offering readers a foundational technique for nurturing the very roots of their breathful existence. Step-by-step instructions and immersive guided practices empower individuals to not only understand but actively cultivate diaphragmatic breathing. It becomes more than just a skill; it transforms into a tool for stress reduction, emotional balance, and a harmonious connection with the self.

Diaphragmatic breathing, often referred to as abdominal or belly breathing, becomes a profound journey into the core of one's being. Readers are guided to explore the expansive movement of the diaphragm, the deep inhalations that fill the lungs, and the slow, deliberate exhalations that release tension. Beyond the physiological benefits, diaphragmatic breathing becomes a mindful exploration of the breathful roots, grounding individuals in the present moment. The section unfolds as an experiential guide, allowing readers to not only grasp the concept but to embody the essence of diaphragmatic breathing.

4.2 Box Breathing and Variations: The Rhythmic Dance of Equanimity

Box breathing, a structured breath technique, is unveiled as a rhythmic dance that balances the symphony of the autonomic nervous system. Readers are guided through the intricate steps of inhalation, holding, exhalation, and resting, discovering how this structured pattern orchestrates a sense of calm and centeredness. Variations of box breathing, like unique notes in a melody, offer flexibility to accommodate diverse preferences and evolving needs. What emerges is not just a technique; it's a personalized breathful practice for harmonizing the mind and body.

The exploration of box breathing becomes a journey into the art of cultivating equanimity—the ability to maintain emotional balance and poise in the face of life's fluctuations. Each phase of the breath becomes a conscious act, a moment of intentional presence. Readers are not merely instructed on how to perform box breathing; they are invited to feel the ebb and flow of each breath, to synchronize with the rhythm of their own equilibrium. The variations of box breathing add layers to this breathful symphony, allowing individuals to tailor their practice to suit different emotional states and situations.

4.3 Mindful Breathing for Stress Reduction: Breathful Resilience in Life's Orchestra

Stress, an inevitable melody in life's orchestra, becomes an opportunity for transformation through mindful breathing. This section delves deep into specific breath practices meticulously designed to reduce stress and foster relaxation. From swift resets in high-pressure situations to more extended practices promoting sustained well-being, readers are bestowed with a repertoire of tools for navigating life's intricate compositions with greater ease. Stress ceases to be a dissonant note; instead, it becomes a part of the breathful symphony of resilience.

The exploration of breathful resilience goes beyond theoretical knowledge, inviting readers to actively engage in practices that fortify their inner resources. Stress reduction becomes an art—a delicate dance between breath and awareness. Readers are guided through moments of rapid breathful resets, akin to tuning an instrument in the midst of a cacophonous performance. The section becomes a sanctuary for individuals seeking refuge from the demands of a hectic life, offering not just a theoretical understanding of stress reduction but a lived experience of breathful resilience.

C. Integrating Breath Awareness into Daily Routines

4.1 Mindful Breathing at Work: The Breathful Cornerstone of Professional Presence

The workplace, often a bustling stage of challenges, becomes an arena where mindful breathing takes center stage. Whether grappling with tight deadlines or navigating intricate interpersonal dynamics, readers discover the seamless integration of mindful breathing into their professional routines. Practical tips transcend theoretical understanding, empowering individuals to cultivate a more mindful, focused, and resilient approach to their professional responsibilities. The breath becomes not just an involuntary response but a conscious and intentional ally in the pursuit of professional presence.

The workplace, with its myriad challenges and demands, transforms into a canvas for the breathful expression of professional presence. From the initial moments of entering the workspace to navigating high-pressure meetings, readers are guided on how to infuse each professional activity with the rhythm of mindful breathing. The breathful cornerstone of professional presence

is not just about staying calm amidst challenges; it's about actively contributing to the workplace environment with a centered and focused mind. This section serves as a beacon for individuals seeking to navigate the complexities of the professional world with grace and mindfulness.

4.2 Mindful Breathing in Relationships: The Breathful Weave of Connection

Healthy relationships thrive on the threads of presence and communication. This section unfurls the potential of mindful breathing to enhance the quality of connections with others. From the art of active listening to navigating the delicate dance of conflicts, readers learn to infuse their relationships with the calming and centering influence of mindful breath awareness. It's not just about understanding; it's about actively participating in the breathful weave that fosters deeper connections and understanding.

The exploration of mindful breathing in relationships becomes a journey into the heart of connection—a breathful weave that transcends words and gestures. Readers are not just provided with theoretical insights; they are immersed in experiential exercises that invite them to actively engage in breathful communication. The breath becomes a silent language, fostering empathy, understanding, and a profound sense of shared presence. This section is a testament to the transformative power of mindful breathing in nurturing meaningful and authentic connections.

4.3 Sustaining Breath Awareness Beyond Formal Practice: The Breathful Continuum

The ultimate goal isn't confined to the moments of formal breath practice; it's about carrying the heightened awareness cultivated through breathful practices into every facet of life. Readers are not merely encouraged but guided to view breath awareness not as a separate activity but as a continuous thread weaving through the very fabric of their experiences. The breath becomes the silent orchestrator, guiding individuals through the symphony of their lives. By the conclusion of this chapter, individuals are not just equipped but inspired to sustain a heightened state of awareness through the rhythmic dance of their breath—a breathful continuum that transforms existence into a mindful masterpiece.

The breathful continuum is more than a concept; it's an invitation to live each moment with a heightened sense of awareness. From the mundane to the extraordinary, readers are encouraged to perceive the breath as a constant companion, guiding them through the ever-changing landscapes of life. Practical tips and reflective exercises ensure that breath awareness becomes an integrated aspect of one's being, rather than a compartmentalized practice. The breathful continuum is an ode to the perpetual dance of existence, where each breath becomes a note in the symphony of mindfulness.

As the exploration of mindful breathing unfolds, readers are invited into a realm where each breath becomes a note in the symphony of awareness. This extended chapter isn't just a guide; it's an immersive experience, inviting individuals to not only understand but actively participate in the breathful art of living.

Chapter Five: Embracing the Present Moment

A. The Art of Being Present

5.1 Presence in Conversation and Connection: The Dance of Mindful Connection

In the intricate dance of human connection, true intimacy is born from the art of being fully present in conversations. This section immerses readers in the nuances of mindful listening, transcending the surface of communication to foster genuine connections. Practical exercises, akin to dance steps, guide individuals in cultivating a profound sense of presence, allowing them to attune to the subtle rhythms of verbal and non-verbal communication. The dance of mindful connection unfolds, enriching interactions and nurturing relationships with authenticity and depth.

As individuals embark on the journey of mindful connection, they are invited to listen not only with their ears but with their hearts. The art of being present in conversations becomes a sacred act, where undivided attention is the currency of connection. Through exercises that explore deep listening and empathetic responses, readers learn to navigate the dance of mindful connection with grace. The result is not just dialogue; it's a shared experience where presence becomes the glue that binds hearts.

5.2 Mindful Observation of Nature and Surroundings: Nature's Silent Teachings

Nature, a silent sage, becomes a potent teacher in the practice of mindfulness. This section is an exploration into the transformative impact of mindfully observing the natural world. Through guided exercises, readers embark on a sensory journey, immersing themselves in the intricate details, colors, and sounds that surround them. Nature, in all its splendor, becomes a sacred canvas for experiencing the richness of the present moment—a masterclass in mindful awareness.

In the tapestry of nature, individuals discover a mirror reflecting the beauty of mindfulness. From the gentle rustle of leaves to the vibrant hues of a sunset, each element becomes a lesson in presence. Through guided observations, readers attune their senses to the subtleties of nature, realizing that the present moment is not a destination but a continuous unfolding. This connection with nature becomes a wellspring of mindfulness, a reminder that the art of being present extends beyond human interactions to encompass the entire universe.

5.3 Present-Moment Joy and Contentment: Savoring Life's Symphony

Joy, a melody of the soul, is not a distant destination but a quality embedded in the present moment. This segment delves into the symbiotic relationship between mindfulness and joy, highlighting the cultivation of contentment through an awareness of life's simple pleasures. By savoring the richness of each moment, individuals become composers of their own symphony, discovering a profound sense of fulfillment in the tapestry of their daily lives.

In the orchestra of life, individuals learn to conduct the music of joy by savoring the present moment. Through exercises that explore gratitude, appreciation, and mindfulness of everyday activities, readers become attuned to the subtle notes of happiness woven into the fabric of their lives. The pursuit of joy transforms from a distant quest to an intimate dance with the present, where each step is a celebration of life's inherent beauty. This chapter becomes a guide for readers to compose their symphony of joy, recognizing that the score is written in the language of mindful awareness.

B. Letting Go of Past Regrets and Future Worries

5.1 Mindful Release of Regret and Guilt: The Alchemy of Self-Compassion

Regret and guilt, heavy anchors of the past, hinder the journey to an awakened life. Mindfulness, an alchemical force, offers a transformative path to release these burdens through the elixir of self-compassion and forgiveness. Readers embark on a journey of self-discovery, exploring practices that gently unravel the knots of regret, creating spaciousness for healing and self-love to blossom.

As individuals navigate the terrain of the past, they discover that self-compassion is the antidote to regret and guilt. Through mindfulness practices that cultivate a kind and non-judgmental awareness of one's own experiences, readers learn to extend the same compassion to themselves that they would offer to a dear friend. The alchemy of self-compassion becomes a healing balm, soothing the wounds of the past and paving the way for a liberated present. This section is an invitation to embark on a journey of self-forgiveness, recognizing that the present moment is the canvas upon which a new story can be painted.

5.2 Overcoming Anxiety About the Future: Navigating the Sea of Uncertainty

The future, a vast sea of uncertainties, often eclipses the joy of the present. This section charts a mindful course for navigating the turbulent waters of future worries. Through cognitive techniques and mindfulness practices, readers learn to sail with a grounded and composed mindset, fostering resilience and a sense of readiness for whatever waves may come. The sea of uncertainty becomes not a threat but a canvas for the mindful sailor to navigate with grace.

In the voyage through future worries, individuals discover that mindfulness is the compass that guides them through the sea of uncertainty. Through practical techniques that include visualization, breath awareness, and present-moment anchoring, readers cultivate an inner resilience that transcends the fear of the unknown. The future becomes not a source of anxiety but an uncharted adventure, and the present moment becomes the anchor that grounds individuals amidst the ebb and flow of time. This chapter becomes a testament to the empowering nature of mindfulness in transforming the relationship with the future, reminding readers that the present is the vessel through which they navigate the vast expanse of possibilities.

5.3 The Freedom of Now: Liberation in Present Awareness

In the present moment, a profound sense of freedom unfurls its wings. This chapter crescendos with a reflection on the liberation that comes from letting go of the shackles of the past and the anxieties of the future. Readers are invited to embrace the boundless possibilities that unfold when one lives fully in the present, experiencing the freedom that arises from mindful awareness. The chapter concludes as a poetic ode to the transformative power of now—a canvas where the art of mindful living paints the strokes of liberation.

As individuals stand at the threshold of the present, they realize that freedom is not a destination but a way of being. Through mindfulness practices that emphasize present-moment awareness, readers are guided to shed the burdens of yesterday and tomorrow, stepping into the canvas of the now with open hearts and liberated spirits. This concluding chapter becomes a beacon, reminding individuals that the key to freedom lies not in the distant horizons of time but in the sacred dance of the present—a dance where each step is a celebration of the infinite possibilities that unfold when one lives with mindful intention. The freedom of now becomes not just a concept but a lived experience, and readers are encouraged to take this newfound sense of liberation into the chapters that follow, weaving it into the fabric of their awakened lives.

C. Finding Joy in the Now

5.1 Cultivating Gratitude: A Symphony of Appreciation

In the tapestry of mindful living, gratitude emerges as a vibrant thread weaving through the present moment. This section invites readers to cultivate gratitude as a transformative practice, a symphony of appreciation that resonates with the heart of joy. Through interactive exercises and reflective prompts, individuals embark on a journey of acknowledging and savoring the abundance that exists in the ordinary. Gratitude becomes the melody that harmonizes with the rhythm of the present, inviting joy to dance in its cadence.

Embracing Gratitude as a Way of Being

Gratitude transcends a mere expression of thanks; it becomes a way of being. Readers delve into the essence of gratitude, understanding how it extends beyond external circumstances to shape one's internal landscape. By embracing gratitude as a fundamental orientation, individuals learn to navigate life with an open heart, attuned to the myriad blessings that unfold in each moment.

Gratitude Journaling: Nurturing the Seed of Joy

A practical aspect of cultivating gratitude involves the art of journaling. Readers are guided in establishing a gratitude journal—a sacred space where daily reflections on moments of thankfulness are recorded. Through the consistent practice of acknowledging and documenting gratitude, individuals witness the gradual blossoming of joy as the seeds of appreciation take root and flourish.

Gratitude in Challenging Moments: A Catalyst for Resilience

The true test of gratitude lies in its application during challenging moments. This section explores how cultivating gratitude becomes a potent catalyst for resilience. By reframing difficulties as opportunities for growth and learning, individuals discover the transformative power of gratitude in navigating life's inevitable ups and downs. Gratitude becomes a guiding light, illuminating the path through adversity.

5.2 Mindful Pleasure and Enjoyment: The Art of Sensory Celebration

Pleasure, often overlooked in the rush of daily life, becomes a focal point in the exploration of joy. This segment encourages readers to engage in the art of mindful pleasure and enjoyment—a sensory celebration that enlivens the present moment. Through experiential exercises, individuals learn to heighten their awareness of pleasurable sensations, whether through taste, touch, sight, sound, or smell.

Savoring the Present: Mindful Eating and Drinking

A foundational aspect of mindful pleasure is found in the simple yet profound act of eating and drinking. Readers are guided in the practice of mindful consumption, savoring each bite and sip with deliberate attention. By immersing themselves fully in the sensory experience of nourishment, individuals discover a source of joy that emanates from the present culinary moment.

Sensory Awareness Meditation: A Journey of Mindful Presence

The exploration of pleasure extends beyond external stimuli to the internal realm of sensations. This section introduces sensory awareness meditation—an experiential journey that guides readers to explore and appreciate the richness of their bodily sensations. By mindfully attending to the present-moment experience, individuals uncover a treasury of joy within the sensory tapestry of their own bodies.

Mindful Pleasure in Creativity and Play

Joy flourishes in the fields of creativity and play. Here, readers discover the transformative potential of engaging in creative endeavors and playful activities with mindful awareness. Whether through art, music, writing, or other forms of expression, individuals learn to infuse their creative pursuits with a sense of joy that arises from being fully present in the act of creation.

5.3 Savoring Life's Simple Pleasures: A Banquet of Mindful Delight

Life's banquet is replete with simple pleasures waiting to be discovered and savored. This section invites readers to partake in the art of savoring—deliberately lingering in the beauty of ordinary moments.

Through mindful engagement with daily activities, such as walking, bathing, or spending time in nature, individuals learn to extract the exquisite flavors of joy inherent in the seemingly mundane.

The Beauty of Ordinary Moments: Mindful Walking and Being

Walking becomes a sacred journey when undertaken with mindful awareness. Readers are encouraged to explore the art of mindful walking, where each step becomes a dance of presence. By savoring the sensations of movement and the surrounding environment, individuals cultivate a deep connection with the present moment, discovering joy in the simplicity of one step at a time.

Mindful Being in Nature: A Symphony of Connection

Nature, a timeless source of inspiration, becomes a canvas for mindful delight. This part explores the joy that arises from mindfully immersing oneself in the natural world. Through guided exercises, individuals learn to appreciate the intricate details of flora and fauna, the soothing cadence of rustling leaves, and the symphony of sounds that compose the melody of nature.

Mindful Bathing: A Ritual of Refreshment and Presence

Bathing, typically a routine activity, is transformed into a ritual of refreshment and presence through mindfulness. Readers are guided in the practice of mindful bathing, where each sensation—the warmth of water, the scent of soap, the touch of hands—is embraced with full attention. The bathroom becomes a sanctuary of joy, and the act of bathing unfolds as a mindful celebration of self-care.

Chapter Six: Nurturing Mindful Relationships

In the intricate tapestry of human connection, mindful relationships stand as the golden threads weaving profound understanding, empathy, and compassion. This chapter explores the depth of mindful relationships, delving into the art of communication, the cultivation of empathy and compassion, and the strengthening of connections through mindful presence.

A. Mindful Communication

6.1 The Role of Listening in Communication

Communication, often seen as mere words exchanged, transforms into an art form when infused with mindfulness. The heartbeat of this art is mindful listening—an immersive experience that transcends the surface. Here, we embark on a journey to unravel the transformative power of truly listening. It goes beyond the auditory realm; it is about suspending judgments, fully engaging, and empathetically understanding. Practical exercises become stepping stones, guiding readers to develop the art of mindful listening—a skill that lays the foundation for authentic and profound connections.

The Symphony of Mindful Listening: Beyond Words

Mindful listening isn't just about hearing words; it's about attuning to the unspoken, the nuances that dance beneath the surface. In this exploration, readers learn to decipher the subtleties in verbal and non-verbal communication. The symphony of mindful listening becomes a melody that resonates at the core of relationships, fostering a deep and harmonious connection.

Creating Sacred Spaces for Dialogue

Communication becomes sacred when approached with mindfulness. This section introduces the concept of creating sacred spaces for dialogue—environments where openness and vulnerability thrive. Through guided practices, individuals learn to establish a mindful space for communication, transcending the mundane and allowing for genuine and meaningful exchanges.

6.2 Expressing Yourself Mindfully

Mindfulness extends its gentle touch to the way we express ourselves. Here, we delve into the art of mindful speech—an eloquent dance of words that flows with clarity, kindness, and intention. Readers embark on a journey to align their words with their inner state, cultivating harmony and authenticity in their communication. Mindful expression transforms into a vehicle for building trust, deepening connections, and creating a resonance of understanding.

The Dance of Mindful Expression: Words as Energy

Communication is an exchange of energy, and mindful expression becomes a dance of intentionality. This section explores how words, when chosen with care and awareness, carry a vibrational resonance that transcends the literal meaning. Readers discover the transformative power of infusing their expressions with mindfulness, turning each conversation into a mindful dance of connection.

The Ripple Effect of Mindful Communication

The impact of mindful expression extends far beyond the immediate interaction. Here, we reflect on the ripple effect of mindful communication—a ripple that reaches into the recesses of relationships and beyond. Through contemplative insights, readers recognize the far-reaching consequences of their words, fostering a conscious approach to communication that contributes to the collective harmony of the world.

6.3 Resolving Conflicts with Presence

Conflict, often perceived as a disruptive force, reveals its potential for growth when approached with mindful awareness. In this section, we navigate the delicate terrain of conflict resolution, guided by the compass of presence. Readers embark on a step-by-step journey, learning to approach disagreements with calmness, understanding, and a profound awareness of the present moment. Mindful conflict resolution becomes an opportunity for transformation, fostering not only resolution but the emergence of stronger and more resilient connections.

The Alchemy of Mindful Conflict Resolution

Conflict resolution becomes an alchemical process when infused with mindfulness. We explore the transformative power of approaching conflicts as opportunities for growth. Through practical strategies and contemplative practices, individuals learn to transmute the raw elements of disagreement into the gold of understanding, creating a foundation for deeper and more authentic relationships.

Embracing Discomfort: The Gateway to Connection

Conflict often carries discomfort, but within that discomfort lies the gateway to profound connection. Here, readers delve into the art of embracing discomfort as a means to understanding and connection. Through mindful exploration of the emotions that arise during conflicts, individuals learn to navigate the storm with grace, transforming moments of tension into catalysts for deeper understanding.

B. Building Empathy and Compassion

6.1 Understanding Empathy in Mindful Relationships

Empathy, the bridge that connects hearts, becomes a focal point in the landscape of mindful relationships. In this section, we delve into the essence of empathy—tuning into the emotions of others with genuine care and understanding. Readers embark on a journey of empathetic practices, cultivating the capacity to share in the joys and sorrows of those around them. Empathy becomes a cornerstone of emotional connection, forging bonds that transcend the surface of everyday interactions.

The Art of Emotional Resonance

Empathy is an art—an intricate dance of emotional resonance. Here, readers explore the nuances of empathetic connection, learning to attune their emotional frequencies to the experiences of others. Through practical exercises, individuals develop the skill of embodying emotional understanding, fostering an environment where each person feels seen and heard.

Compassion-Fueled Listening

Empathy blossoms into its fullest expression through compassionate listening. This segment explores how mindful relationships are nurtured when empathy is infused with the balm of compassion. Readers learn the art of listening not only with their ears but with their hearts, creating a space where understanding is accompanied by the warmth of benevolence.

6.2 Compassion as a Natural Outcome of Mindfulness

Mindfulness, as a gentle current, naturally leads to the shores of compassion. Here, we deepen our understanding of the inseparable link between mindfulness and compassion. Readers discover that a mindful way of being naturally fosters greater kindness, consideration, and understanding. Compassion becomes not just an individual practice but a collective force that shapes the dynamics of relationships and transforms the emotional landscape.

The Ecology of Compassion: Nurturing the Relationship Ecosystem

Compassion, when integrated into the ecosystem of relationships, becomes a sustaining force. This section explores the interconnected web of compassion that envelops individuals, couples, families, and communities. Through contemplative insights, readers gain an appreciation for how acts of compassion reverberate through the relationship ecosystem, creating a nourishing and supportive environment.

The Ripple Effect of Compassion

The impact of compassion extends beyond the immediate circle of relationships, creating ripples in the broader community. Here, we reflect on the far-reaching consequences of cultivating compassion in relationships—a ripple that extends its gentle touch to the collective consciousness. Through meditative contemplation, readers recognize their role as agents of compassion, contributing to the co-creation of a more compassionate and interconnected world.

6.3 Extending Kindness to Others and Yourself

Kindness, the language of mindfulness, becomes the cornerstone of nurturing mindful relationships. In this segment, we explore how cultivating kindness towards oneself and others enriches the tapestry of connections. Through self-compassion practices and intentional acts of kindness, readers learn to create an atmosphere of warmth and understanding. Kindness becomes a currency that circulates freely in the economy of relationships, fostering an environment where each person is valued and appreciated.

The Self-Kindness Revolution

Kindness begins at home—with oneself. Here, readers embark on a revolution of self-kindness, recognizing that a compassionate relationship with oneself lays the foundation for mindful connections with others. Through practical exercises and reflective practices, individuals learn to cultivate self-kindness as a source of strength, resilience, and a wellspring of benevolence that spills over into their relationships.

The Ripple of Kindness: A Tapestry of Connection

Kindness, when woven into the fabric of relationships, creates a tapestry of connection that is both intricate and resilient. This part reflects on the ripple effect of kindness—a ripple that extends from the individual to the collective, fostering a culture of benevolence and consideration. Through contemplative exploration, readers witness the transformative power of kindness in shaping the relational landscape.

C. Strengthening Connections Through Presence

6.1 Quality Time and Mindful Presence

In a world fraught with distractions, quality time becomes a precious gift in the cultivation of mindful relationships. This section emphasizes the importance of dedicating focused and mindful presence to loved ones. Readers learn that through mindful rituals and shared activities, they can deepen connections by being fully present in the moments they share.

The Art of Mindful Rituals

Rituals become sacred when approached with mindfulness. Here, readers discover the art of creating mindful rituals that deepen connections. Whether through shared meals, daily check-ins, or other intentional practices, individuals learn to infuse everyday moments with mindful awareness. Rituals become a tapestry of shared experiences, weaving a narrative of connection and presence.

Unplugging for Connection

In the digital age, unplugging becomes an essential practice for nurturing mindful relationships. This part explores the art of disconnecting from technology to reconnect with loved ones. Through practical tips and contemplative insights, readers learn to create spaces of digital silence, allowing for genuine and uninterrupted connection in the presence of one another.

6.2 Shared Mindfulness Practices

Mutual mindfulness practices emerge as a powerful bond in relationships. In this section, we explore how couples, families, and friends can embark on mindfulness journeys together. Whether through meditation, nature walks, or mindful meals, shared practices become opportunities for bonding and co-creating a mindful way of life.

The Dance of Shared Presence

Shared mindfulness practices become a dance of presence—an intimate exploration of being together in the present moment. Here, readers learn that through joint activities that foster mindfulness, relationships deepen organically. The chapter provides practical guidance on initiating shared mindfulness practices, allowing individuals to embark on a journey of co-presence and connection.

Mindful Parenting: Nurturing Connection with Presence

Parenting, a sacred journey, is enriched through mindful presence. This segment explores the art of mindful parenting, guiding individuals to navigate the joys and challenges of raising children with intentional awareness. Through practical insights and reflective practices, readers learn to cultivate a mindful presence that nourishes the parent-child relationship.

6.3 The Ripple Effect of Mindful Relationships

The impact of mindful relationships extends far beyond the individuals involved, creating ripples in the broader community. In the concluding segment of this chapter, we reflect on the ripple effect of cultivating mindfulness in relationships. Through meditative contemplation, readers recognize their role as contributors to a more compassionate and interconnected world. The chapter concludes with a profound exploration of how mindful relationships can serve as catalysts for positive change, creating waves of connection that ripple through the collective consciousness.

Chapter Seven: Mindful Practices for Inner Peace

In the sacred realms of inner exploration, Chapter Seven unfolds as a profound journey into mindful practices that serve as anchors for cultivating lasting inner peace. Through an immersive exploration of meditation, mindfulness exercises, and the integration of presence into daily life, readers embark on a transformative odyssey toward the serene landscapes within.

A. Meditation and Mindfulness Exercises

7.1 Exploring Various Meditation Techniques

Meditation, the sanctum of inner discovery, beckons readers into a rich tapestry of contemplative practices. This section deepens the exploration, unveiling a myriad of meditation techniques, each a unique portal to self-awareness. From the gentle cadence of mindfulness of breath to the expansive embrace of loving-kindness meditation, readers are gently guided through diverse approaches. This nuanced exploration invites individuals to resonate with the methods that harmonize most profoundly with the whispers of their unique journey.

The Symphony of Silence: Navigating Meditation Styles

Meditation is a symphony of silence, with each technique playing a distinctive note. Here, readers traverse the intricate melodies of various meditation styles. From Zen mindfulness to transcendental practices, the chapter becomes a guidebook for the musical landscape of meditation, allowing individuals to compose their own harmonious journey.

Sacred Spaces of Meditation

Meditation transcends physical spaces; it is an inner pilgrimage. This section introduces the concept of sacred spaces within, where meditation becomes a profound dialogue with the self. Through evocative imagery and reflective practices, individuals learn to create inner sanctuaries, fostering an environment conducive to deep meditation and inner exploration.

7.2 Mindfulness in Movement: Yoga and Walking

In the rhythmic dance of mindful movement, the chapter expands to embrace the integration of mindfulness into the body's graceful gestures. Beyond the stillness of seated meditation, mindful movement becomes a gateway to embodied presence. The spotlight turns to yoga and walking meditation, inviting readers to synchronize breath with movement. Through intentional steps and postures, individuals learn to dance with mindfulness, forging a harmonious connection between the corporeal and the ethereal.

Embodied Presence: The Art of Mindful Movement

Mindful movement is an art—an artistry of breath and motion. Here, readers delve into the nuances of embodying mindfulness in every step and stretch. From the meditative flow of yoga asanas to the contemplative rhythm of walking meditation, the chapter unfolds as a canvas for exploring the exquisite beauty of mindful movement.

Nature as a Moving Meditation

In the embrace of nature, movement becomes a sacred dance of connection. This part explores the transformative impact of nature-infused movement. Through guided exercises, individuals learn to engage with the natural world as a moving meditation, fostering a sense of communion with the earth, sky, and the gentle rustle of leaves.

7.3 Developing a Personal Meditation Routine

Consistency, the heartbeat of mindfulness, resonates throughout this section as readers are gently guided to forge a personalized meditation routine. The chapter becomes a compass, navigating through the landscape of daily life to build a sustainable meditation habit. Practical tips emerge as steppingstones, empowering individuals to weave mindfulness seamlessly into the fabric of their daily existence.

Rituals of Presence: Crafting a Personal Sanctuary

Meditation transforms into a ritual of presence—a sacred sanctuary within the rhythm of life. Here, readers explore the art of crafting personal rituals that prepare the mind for meditation. Through rituals of sacred space, intention-setting, and gentle transitions, individuals learn to create a conducive environment for diving into the depths of meditation.

Mindful Beginnings and Endings

The transition into and out of meditation is a threshold of significance. This segment unfolds as a mindful guide to the beginnings and endings of meditation sessions. Through contemplative practices, individuals cultivate an awareness that transcends the temporal boundaries of meditation, infusing the entire day with the gentle fragrance of mindfulness.

B. Creating a Personal Mindfulness Routine

7.1 Designing a Daily Mindfulness Schedule

Mindfulness, an ever-present companion, beckons readers to design a daily schedule infused with its essence. The exploration transcends formal meditation sessions, extending into the realm of everyday life. This section becomes a tapestry of mindful moments woven into routine activities, cultivating a pervasive sense of awareness that transcends the mundane.

Mindful Mornings: A Symphony of Beginnings

The morning becomes a canvas for mindful beginnings. Here, readers explore the art of designing mindful mornings—a symphony of awakening the senses, setting intentions, and embracing the unfolding day with awareness. Through practical insights, individuals learn to infuse the early hours with mindfulness, creating a foundation for a day imbued with presence.

Mindfulness Throughout the Day: A Dance of Awareness

Mindfulness isn't confined to specific hours; it's a dance that accompanies every moment. This part unfolds as a guide to integrating mindfulness into work and leisure, transforming routine activities into mindful endeavors. From mindful work breaks to savoring leisure moments with full awareness, individuals learn to navigate the demands of life with grace and unwavering presence.

7.2 Integrating Mindfulness into Work and Leisure

Work and leisure, often viewed as separate realms, converge in the landscape of mindful living. This section offers tailored strategies for infusing mindfulness into professional responsibilities and leisure activities. The chapter becomes a companion, guiding individuals to navigate the complexities of work with a mindful approach, fostering balance and harmony.

Mindful Workspaces: Cultivating Presence in Professional Settings

The workplace transforms into a canvas for mindful expression. Here, readers delve into the art of creating mindful workspaces—environments that nurture focused attention, creativity, and well-being. Through practical tips, individuals learn to infuse their professional responsibilities with mindfulness, cultivating a sense of purpose and presence in the midst of work.

Leisure as Meditation: Savoring Moments of Rest

Leisure activities become an opportunity for mindful rejuvenation. This part explores the art of savoring moments of rest with full awareness. Through contemplative practices, individuals learn to transform leisure into a meditative experience, deepening their connection with the present moment and finding solace in the simplicity of being.

7.3 Overcoming Challenges in Establishing a Routine

Challenges, like gentle storms, dot the landscape of establishing a mindfulness routine. This section stands as a beacon of resilience, addressing common obstacles with practical solutions and transformative mindset shifts. Readers are empowered not only to overcome setbacks but to view challenges as opportunities for growth on their journey to inner peace.

Embracing Imperfection: A Compassionate Approach

Imperfection becomes a canvas for compassion. Here, readers explore the art of embracing imperfection in the mindfulness journey. Through reflective practices, individuals learn to approach setbacks with a compassionate heart, recognizing that the path to inner peace is adorned with the colors of resilience, self-compassion, and a gentle acceptance of the ebb and flow of life.

Transformative Shifts in Perspective

Obstacles morph into opportunities for transformation when viewed through a mindful lens. This part becomes a guide to shifting perspectives, empowering individuals to see challenges not as roadblocks but as catalysts for growth. Through contemplative insights, readers navigate the terrain of setbacks with a newfound resilience and an unwavering commitment to the path of inner peace.

C. Harnessing Inner Peace Amidst Chaos

7.1 Mindfulness in Stressful Situations

Stress, an ever-present companion, becomes an arena for the transformative dance of mindfulness. This section unveils specific techniques tailored for navigating stressful situations with grace and composure. Through the alchemy of breath awareness, visualization, and present-moment focus, readers discover the antidote to stress within themselves, cultivating a sanctuary of tranquility amidst life's tumult.

The Breath as a Lifeline: Navigating Stress with Awareness

The breath emerges as a lifeline in the storm of stress. Here, readers delve into the transformative power of breath awareness as a potent tool for navigating turbulent situations. Through guided practices, individuals learn to anchor themselves in the present moment, cultivating a reservoir of calm that serves as a compass in the face of life's storms.

Mindful Responses to Stress: A Symphony of Equanimity

Stressful situations become a canvas for the symphony of mindful responses. This segment unfolds as a guide to cultivating equanimity in the face of chaos. Through mindful responses rooted in acceptance and present-moment awareness, individuals navigate the waves of stress with a composed spirit, fostering a resilient core amidst life's challenges.

7.2 Finding Calm in the Midst of Turbulence

Life's turbulence, rather than a hurdle, becomes an invitation to deepen the practice of inner peace. This section explores the mindful approach to facing challenges and uncertainties. Through the alchemy of acceptance, equanimity, and non-resistance, readers learn to find a calm center within, fostering a sense of stability regardless of external circumstances.

The Stillness Within Chaos: A Mindful Perspective

Within the storm, there is a sanctuary of stillness. Here, readers explore the art of adopting a mindful perspective in the midst of turbulence. Through contemplative insights, individuals learn to view challenges not as disruptions but as opportunities for deepening their practice of inner peace. Life's uncertainties become a canvas for the brushstrokes of mindfulness, creating a masterpiece of resilience.

The Dance of Acceptance and Transformation

Acceptance becomes the dance partner in the choreography of inner peace. This part unfolds as a guide to embracing challenges with a spirit of acceptance, recognizing that within acceptance lies the seed of transformation. Through transformative practices, readers learn to dance with the rhythm of acceptance, fostering a sense of peace that transcends external circumstances.

7.3 The Transformative Power of Inner Peace

The chapter crescendos with a reflection on the transformative power of inner peace. Readers are invited to witness the ripple effects of cultivating serenity in their lives and in the lives of those around them. The journey of mindfulness becomes a profound exploration of the self, leading to a more peaceful, purposeful, and fulfilled existence.

The Ripple of Inner Peace: A Tapestry of Tranquility

Inner peace becomes a tapestry woven into the fabric of existence. This segment reflects on the ripple effect of inner peace—a ripple that extends from the individual to the collective, fostering a culture of tranquility and understanding. Through contemplative exploration, readers witness the transformative power of inner peace in shaping not only their personal narratives but also the collective consciousness.

Beyond the Self: The Collective Impact of Inner Peace

The transformative power of inner peace extends beyond individual lives, creating waves of positive change in the broader community. In this part, we delve into the collective impact of inner peace—a ripple that resonates through relationships, communities, and the world. Through meditative contemplation, readers recognize their role as agents of positive change, contributing to the co-creation of a more peaceful and interconnected world.

Chapter Eight: Mindful Decision-Making and Action

In the intricate dance of decision-making and intentional action, Chapter Eight unfolds as a labyrinth of wisdom, guiding readers through the profound intersection of mindfulness, choices, and the consequences that ripple through the tapestry of life. Here, we embark on an odyssey that transcends the mere act of decision-making, diving into the art of deliberation, the consequences of mindful choices, intentional action, and the transformative impact of mindful leadership.

A. Applying Mindfulness to Choices

8.1 Mindful Decision-Making Principles

Mindfulness, the silent orchestrator of our consciousness, extends its gentle touch to the realm of choices. This segment delves into the foundational principles of mindful decision-making—a compass that guides individuals to navigate the intricate landscapes of options with grace and clarity. Through a nuanced exploration of present-moment awareness, clarity of intention, and alignment with core values, readers cultivate a discerning mindset that becomes the compass for choices grounded in mindfulness.

Present-Moment Awareness: The Fertile Ground of Decision-Making

Every choice unfolds in the fertile soil of the present moment. Here, readers traverse the nuanced landscape of present-moment awareness, learning to harness the power of now in their decision-making process. Through mindful practices and contemplative exercises, individuals develop an acute sensitivity to the currents of the present, allowing decisions to blossom with a profound sense of presence.

Clarity of Intention: Illuminating the Path of Choice

Intentions become the guiding stars in the constellation of choices. This section becomes a celestial navigation guide, unraveling the art of fostering clarity of intention. Through introspective practices and reflective inquiry, individuals learn to illuminate the path of choice with intentions that resonate with their deepest aspirations, creating a tapestry of decisions woven with purpose.

8.2 The Art of Deliberation

Decision-making, a delicate tapestry woven with threads of consequence, requires the art of deliberation. This part unfolds as a guide to the mindful approach of considering options, weighing consequences, and discerning the most aligned choice. Through practical exercises that invite patience and introspection, readers cultivate the art of deliberation, ensuring decisions emerge not from haste but from a mindful consideration of possibilities.

Patience in Decision-Making: Nurturing the Seeds of Wisdom

In the garden of decision-making, patience becomes the soil in which the seeds of wisdom sprout. Here, readers explore the art of patient deliberation, learning to nurture the seeds of wisdom through a slow and deliberate consideration of options. Through mindfulness practices that enhance patience, individuals navigate the intricate terrain of decision-making with a grounded spirit.

Clarity Amidst Complexity: Illuminating the Crossroads

The crossroads of decision-making can be daunting, but mindfulness becomes the lantern that illuminates the path. This segment becomes a beacon of clarity amidst complexity, guiding readers to discern the most aligned choices. Through contemplative practices that unveil the layers of options, individuals gain a heightened awareness that transcends confusion, fostering decisions bathed in the light of clear discernment.

8.3 The Consequences of Mindful Choices

Every choice, a pebble cast into the pond of existence, creates ripples that touch the shores of our lives and those around us. This section explores the profound consequences of mindful choices, illuminating how these ripples weave through the fabric of well-being. Readers gain insight into the transformative potential of making choices with conscious intention, recognizing that each decision shapes the tapestry of their narrative.

Ripples of Well-Being: The Transformative Tapestry

The consequences of mindful choices become the threads that weave a transformative tapestry of well-being. Here, readers delve into the intricate patterns created by conscious decisions, exploring how these ripples touch aspects of life, from personal growth to relationships. Through reflective practices, individuals witness the transformative potential inherent in every choice, recognizing the power they hold to shape a narrative infused with mindfulness.

Ripple Effect on Relationships: Weaving Connections

Mindful choices, like gentle winds, carry the fragrance of well-being to the relationships that grace our lives. This part becomes a reflection on the ripple effect of mindful choices in the realm of connections. Through contemplative inquiry, readers recognize the impact of their decisions on the well-being of others, fostering a harmonious dance of interconnectedness.

B. Intentional Action and Consequence

8.1 Aligning Actions with Values

Mindful living unfolds as a journey of aligning actions with the compass of deepest values. This section becomes a guiding star, illuminating how mindfulness provides a compass for intentional living. Readers traverse the landscapes of reflection and introspection, discovering the profound sense of purpose that infuses their actions with meaning. The chapter unfolds as an invitation to delve into the depths of one's values, exploring how these core principles can become the guiding force for intentional and mindful living.

Values as a Compass: Navigating the Landscape of Intention

Values become the compass that guides intentional living. Here, readers embark on an exploration of values as the foundational force shaping actions. Through introspective practices and contemplative exercises, individuals learn to navigate the landscapes of intention, ensuring that their actions resonate harmoniously with their core principles.

The Dance of Purpose: Infusing Actions with Meaning

Purpose becomes the melody that infuses actions with meaning. This segment becomes a symphony of intentional living, exploring how mindfulness deepens the connection between actions and purpose. Through contemplative inquiry, individuals learn to dance with purpose, fostering a sense of alignment that transforms actions into a harmonious expression of mindful living.

8.2 Mindful Execution of Tasks and Goals

Execution, the dynamic dance of bringing intentions to life, takes center stage in this section. Here, readers delve into the mindfulness of action, recognizing that being fully present in the process of carrying out tasks and pursuing goals is as crucial as the initial decision-making. The chapter unfolds as a guide to infusing intentionality and focus into actions, fostering a sense of accomplishment and fulfillment in the execution of tasks.

Embodied Presence in Action: The Mindful Choreography

Action becomes a mindful choreography—an embodied presence in the unfolding dance of life. This part becomes a journey into the nuances of being fully present in the execution of tasks and goals. Through mindfulness practices that heighten awareness, individuals learn to embody each action with intentionality, transforming routine tasks into sacred endeavors.

Focused Attention in Goal Pursuit: The Art of Mindful Achievement

The pursuit of goals becomes an art—a canvas for the brushstrokes of focused attention. This segment becomes a guide to the mindfulness of goal pursuit, exploring how individuals can infuse intentionality into their journey of achievement. Through contemplative practices, readers learn to navigate the terrain of goals with unwavering focus, fostering a sense of accomplishment and fulfillment.

8.3 Learning from Consequences with Compassion

In the intricate dance of intentional living, not every step unfolds as expected, and consequences often become the silent teachers on the journey. This section unfolds as an exploration of the art of learning from consequences with compassion rather than judgment. Readers delve into the transformative power of self-compassion in the face of challenges and setbacks. Through mindful reflection, individuals extract valuable lessons from every experience, fostering growth, resilience, and a deeper understanding of the self.

Compassion in Setbacks: Nurturing the Seeds of Growth

Setbacks become fertile ground for growth when approached with a heart of compassion. Here, readers explore the art of cultivating self-compassion in the face of challenges. Through contemplative practices that embrace setbacks as opportunities for learning, individuals nurture the seeds of growth, fostering resilience and a deeper understanding of themselves.

The Wisdom in Reflection: Extracting Lessons from Experience

Reflection becomes the lantern that illuminates the path of wisdom. This part becomes a guide to mindful reflection, exploring how individuals can extract valuable lessons from every experience. Through contemplative practices, readers learn to delve into the nuances of their journey, recognizing that each consequence carries the potential for wisdom and self-discovery.

C. Mindful Leadership and Responsibility

8.1 Mindfulness in Leadership Roles

Leadership, a tapestry woven with threads of influence, benefits profoundly from a mindful approach. This section unfolds as an exploration of the qualities of mindful leadership—compassion, empathy, and the ability to inspire positive change. Readers are guided in integrating mindfulness into their leadership roles, recognizing that leadership extends beyond formal positions to the subtle influence individuals have on those around them.

Compassionate Leadership: Weaving Threads of Influence

Leadership becomes a canvas for compassionate influence—a tapestry woven with threads of empathy and understanding. This part unfolds as a guide to the qualities of mindful leadership, exploring how individuals can infuse their roles with compassion and inspire positive change. Through contemplative practices, readers learn to navigate the complexities of leadership with a heart-centered approach.

Empathy as a Catalyst: Bridging Connections in Leadership

Empathy becomes the catalyst that bridges hearts in leadership. This segment becomes an exploration of the role of empathy in mindful leadership, delving into how leaders can tune into the emotions of others with genuine care and understanding. Through empathetic practices, readers learn to foster a sense of connection and emotional resonance, creating a positive and harmonious influence.

8.2 Navigating Ethical Dilemmas with Mindfulness

Ethical dilemmas, the crossroads where values meet challenges, pose intricate puzzles in decision-making. This section becomes a guiding light in navigating these complexities with mindfulness. Through ethical mindfulness practices, readers learn to approach dilemmas with clarity, integrity, and a deep understanding of the interconnectedness of their choices. The chapter unfolds as an exploration of how mindfulness becomes the compass that guides individuals through the moral intricacies of decision-making.

Clarity in Ethical Decision-Making: The Mindful Compass

Ethical decision-making becomes a mindful compass—an inner guide that illuminates the path of integrity. Here, readers explore the nuances of approaching ethical dilemmas with clarity. Through mindfulness practices that heighten ethical awareness, individuals learn to navigate the complexities of choices, ensuring that their decisions align with their values and contribute to the well-being of all.

The Interconnected Web of Ethics: Mindfulness in Decision-Making

Ethics becomes the interconnected web that binds decisions to the well-being of the collective. This part becomes a reflection on the role of mindfulness in decision-making, recognizing the intricate dance between individual choices and the broader ethical landscape. Through contemplative inquiry, readers gain insight into how their decisions contribute to the interconnected fabric of ethics, fostering a sense of responsibility for the collective well-being.

8.3 Inspiring Others through Mindful Leadership

The chapter crescendos with a reflection on the ripple effect of mindful leadership. Readers are invited to inspire positive change not only through their choices but also through the example they set for others. The mindful leader becomes a catalyst for a more conscious and harmonious world, recognizing that the influence of leadership extends far beyond the individual. Through contemplative exploration, individuals witness the transformative power of mindful leadership, recognizing their role as agents of positive change in the collective tapestry of existence.

Leading by Example: The Ripple of Conscious Influence

Mindful leadership becomes a ripple of conscious influence—a beacon that lights the path for others. This segment unfolds as a reflection on the impact of leading by example, recognizing that the choices and actions of a mindful leader resonate beyond the individual sphere. Through contemplative inquiry, readers delve into the transformative potential of inspiring others through mindful leadership, fostering a culture of conscious influence.

A Harmonious World: The Collective Impact of Mindful Leadership

The transformative power of mindful leadership extends beyond individual lives, creating waves of positive change in the broader community. This part becomes an exploration of the collective impact of mindful leadership—a ripple that resonates through relationships, communities, and the world. Through meditative contemplation, readers recognize their role as agents of positive change, contributing to the co-creation of a more peaceful and interconnected world.

In the grand tapestry of mindful decision-making and action, this chapter invites readers to unravel the threads of choices, consequences, intentional living, and leadership, recognizing that every decision is a brushstroke, every action a note, and every leader a composer in the symphony of mindful existence. As we navigate the realms of mindfulness, may the choices we make, the actions we take, and the leadership we embody create a tapestry that reflects the beauty and wisdom of living with intention and consciousness.

Chapter Nine: Overcoming Challenges with Mindfulness

In the realm of life's inevitable challenges, Chapter Nine unfolds as a sanctuary of resilience, guiding readers through the transformative landscape of mindfulness in overcoming stress, grief, and adversity. Here, we embark on a journey that transcends the mere act of coping, delving into the profound realms of building emotional resilience, embracing impermanence, and transforming pain into growth. As we navigate the intricacies of mindfulness in the face of adversity, may this chapter serve as a compass, offering practical tools and reflective insights to navigate the ebb and flow of life's challenges with grace and strength.

A. Mindfulness as a Coping Mechanism

9.1 Coping with Stress and Anxiety

Stress and anxiety, the shadows that accompany the human experience, find their antidote in the sanctuary of mindfulness. This section becomes a portal into specific mindfulness practices, offering readers practical tools to navigate the tumultuous waters of stress and anxiety. Through contemplative practices that harness the power of breath and present-moment awareness, individuals learn to find calm in the midst of life's storms.

Breath as the Anchor: Navigating the Storms of Stress

In the storm of stress, the breath becomes the anchor that grounds the ship of consciousness. This part becomes an exploration of how mindful breathing practices offer a sanctuary amidst stress and anxiety. Through breath awareness and intentional practices, readers cultivate an inner calm, discovering the transformative potential of using the breath as a constant companion in navigating life's challenges.

Present-Moment Awareness: Dissolving Anxiety in the Now

Anxiety often finds its roots in the uncertain future, but mindfulness offers a refuge in the present moment. This segment becomes a guide to present-moment awareness as a potent tool for dissolving anxiety. Through practices that anchor individuals in the now, readers learn to release the grip of anxious thoughts, fostering a sense of peace in the present.

9.2 Mindfulness in Times of Grief and Loss

Grief and loss, the silent companions in the human journey, unfold as universal experiences that can be profoundly challenging. Mindfulness steps in as a compassionate companion, offering solace in navigating the depths of sorrow. This segment becomes a journey into guided practices and reflections, inviting readers to approach grief with mindfulness. Through practices that honor the pain and invite self-compassion, individuals foster healing and resilience in the face of loss.

Compassion in Grief: Nurturing the Heart Amidst Sorrow

In the landscape of grief, compassion becomes the gentle rain that nurtures the heart. This part unfolds as an exploration of how mindfulness practices invite individuals to approach grief with self-compassion. Through contemplative practices that acknowledge the depth of sorrow, readers learn to navigate the emotional landscape with gentleness, fostering a sense of healing and resilience.

Mindfulness as the Compass: Navigating Loss with Grace

Loss becomes a journey navigated with grace through the compass of mindfulness. Here, readers delve into the transformative power of mindfulness in the face of loss. Through practices that honor the unique experience of grief, individuals learn to navigate the waves of emotions with mindfulness as their guiding light.

9.3 Building Emotional Resilience

Emotional resilience emerges as a cornerstone of well-being, and mindfulness becomes the nurturing soil in which this resilience can flourish. This section explores the intricate dance between mindfulness and emotional resilience, guiding readers to bounce back from adversity with grace and strength. Through practices that cultivate emotional well-being, individuals develop a resilient mindset that becomes a source of strength in the face of life's challenges.

Mindfulness in Emotional Terrain: Cultivating Resilient Soil

Emotions become the terrain through which mindfulness cultivates the soil of resilience. This part becomes an exploration of how mindfulness practices contribute to the development of emotional resilience. Through practices that bring attention to the ebb and flow of emotions, readers learn to cultivate a resilient mindset that allows them to navigate the complex landscape of feelings with grace.

Nurturing Emotional Well-Being: Mindfulness Practices for Resilience

Well-being becomes the blossoming flower nurtured by the waters of mindfulness. This segment becomes a guide to mindfulness practices that nurture emotional well-being. Through practices that foster self-awareness and self-regulation, individuals learn to tend to their emotional landscape, creating a resilient inner garden that blooms amidst life's challenges.

B. Resilience in the Face of Adversity

9.1 Embracing Impermanence and Change

Change, the constant companion of existence, takes center stage in this section as mindfulness offers a perspective that transforms our relationship with it. The mindfulness of impermanence becomes a guiding light, inviting readers to embrace change as a natural part of life. Through contemplative practices that foster acceptance and understanding, individuals develop a resilient mindset that allows them to navigate transitions with greater ease.

Impermanence as the Essence: Embracing the Dance of Change

In the dance of life, impermanence becomes the essence that infuses every step. This part becomes an exploration of how mindfulness practices invite individuals to embrace impermanence and change. Through practices that bring awareness to the transient nature of all things, readers learn to navigate the unfolding dance of life with a resilient spirit.

Mindfulness in Transition: Navigating Change with Ease

Transitions become passages navigated with ease through the lens of mindfulness. Here, readers delve into the transformative power of mindfulness in adapting to challenges. Through practices that foster flexibility and openness, individuals learn to navigate uncertainty with a grounded and composed mindset. Mindfulness becomes the compass that guides individuals through the ever-changing landscapes of life.

9.2 The Role of Mindfulness in Adapting to Challenges

Adaptability emerges as a key component of resilience, and mindfulness becomes the ally that enhances our capacity to adapt to challenges. This section unfolds as a journey into how mindfulness practices foster flexibility and openness. Through practices that heighten awareness and acceptance, readers learn to navigate uncertainty with a grounded and composed mindset, fostering a sense of adaptability in the face of change.

Mindfulness and Flexibility: Navigating the River of Change

Flexibility becomes the vessel that carries individuals through the river of change. This part becomes an exploration of how mindfulness practices enhance adaptability. Through practices that invite individuals to remain present in the face of change, readers develop the flexibility to bend with the winds of uncertainty, fostering resilience during challenges.

Openness in Uncertainty: The Mindful Stance in Adversity

Uncertainty becomes the canvas upon which mindfulness paints the portrait of adaptability. This segment becomes a guide to the role of mindfulness in navigating challenges with
openness. Through practices that invite individuals to approach challenges with a receptive heart, readers learn to embrace the unknown with a sense of curiosity, fostering adaptability in the face of adversity.

9.3 Transforming Pain into Growth

Painful experiences become transformative landscapes when approached with the lens of mindfulness. This section becomes a journey into the mindful perspective on pain, guiding readers to view challenges as opportunities for growth. Through practices that invite introspection and self-compassion, individuals learn to transform pain into wisdom, resilience, and personal evolution.

Mindfulness and Pain: The Alchemy of Transformation

Pain becomes the alchemy of transformation through the lens of mindfulness. This part becomes an exploration of how mindfulness practices invite individuals to approach pain with self-compassion. Through practices that acknowledge the rawness of pain and encourage self-reflection, readers learn to navigate the intricate landscape of suffering, discovering the seeds of growth within.

Wisdom from Pain: Nurturing Resilience Through Mindfulness

Pain becomes the wellspring of wisdom, nurturing resilience through the waters of mindfulness. This segment becomes a guide to mindfulness practices that transform pain into growth. Through practices that invite individuals to extract valuable lessons from their experiences, readers learn to embrace the transformative potential within every challenge.

C. Transforming Challenges into Growth Opportunities

9.1 The Mindful Perspective on Challenges

Challenges cease to be obstacles; they become invitations to growth in this section. Mindfulness reframes our relationship with difficulties, encouraging readers to approach challenges with curiosity and an open heart. Mindfulness practices unfold as tools for uncovering the hidden potential for growth within every challenge.

Curiosity in Difficulty: The Mindful Approach to Challenges

Difficulty becomes a canvas inviting the strokes of curiosity through the lens of mindfulness. This part becomes an exploration of how mindfulness practices encourage individuals to approach challenges with a sense of curiosity. Through practices that invite a non-judgmental and open-hearted stance, readers learn to uncover the layers of growth hidden within every challenge.

Mindfulness as the Guide: Navigating the Labyrinth of Challenges

Challenges become labyrinths navigated with the guiding light of mindfulness. This segment becomes a guide to the mindful perspective on challenges, recognizing that mindfulness practices offer a compass for the journey through difficulties. Through practices that bring attention to the present moment, readers learn to navigate challenges with a steady and mindful presence.

9.2 Finding Meaning and Purpose in Difficulties

Meaning emerges as a powerful motivator in the face of adversity, and mindfulness becomes the torch that illuminates the path to discovering meaning and purpose in difficult circumstances. This section unfolds as a journey into how mindfulness contributes to the discovery of profound meaning even during challenges. Through reflective practices, readers uncover the deeper layers of their experiences, finding profound meaning in the tapestry of difficulties.

Mindfulness and Meaning: Illuminating the Darkness of Challenges

Challenges become canvases illuminated by the light of meaning through the lens of mindfulness. This part becomes an exploration of how mindfulness practices contribute to the discovery of meaning in difficult circumstances. Through practices that invite individuals to explore the deeper layers of their experiences, readers learn to find purpose even during challenges.

Reflective Practices: Unveiling Deeper Layers of Experience

Meaning becomes a tapestry woven from the threads of reflection and introspection. This segment becomes a guide to reflective practices that unveil the deeper layers of experience. Through practices that invite individuals to contemplate their challenges with a discerning eye, readers learn to discover the profound meaning woven into the fabric of their difficulties.

9.3 Resilience and Growth Through Mindfulness

The chapter crescendos with a reflection on the interplay between mindfulness, resilience, and personal growth. Readers are invited to recognize the transformative potential within themselves, acknowledging that the mindful approach to challenges is a journey of continuous growth and evolution.

Mindfulness as the Seed: Nurturing Growth Amidst Challenges

Mindfulness becomes the seed that nurtures growth amidst the challenges of life. This part becomes an exploration of how mindfulness practices contribute to resilience and personal growth. Through practices that invite individuals to meet challenges with an open heart and a present mind, readers learn to cultivate a resilient spirit that blossoms amidst the complexities of life.

Continuous Evolution: The Journey of Mindful Growth

Growth becomes a river that flows continuously through the landscape of mindfulness. This segment becomes a guide to the journey of continuous evolution through mindfulness. Through practices that invite individuals to view challenges as opportunities for learning and transformation, readers recognize that the mindful approach is a path of continuous growth, weaving through the tapestry of existence.

Chapter Ten: The Endless Path of Mindfulness: Navigating Life's Oceans

A. The Eternal Journey of Mindfulness

10.1 Embracing Mindfulness as a Lifelong Odyssey

Mindfulness, a timeless voyage rather than a fixed destination, beckons individuals on an endless odyssey. This section unfolds the philosophy of mindfulness as a lifelong practice, urging readers to embrace the evolving nature of their journey. Through introspection, they're encouraged to perceive mindfulness not as a static achievement but as a continuous exploration, adapting and deepening with each step.

The Odyssey Unveiled: Navigating the Seas of Self-Discovery

In the vast seas of self-discovery, mindfulness acts as the compass guiding the odyssey. This subsection serves as a nautical chart, illustrating how mindfulness practices act as navigational tools in exploring the inner landscapes. Through practices of introspection and self-awareness, readers embark on a transformative journey, unveiling the depths of their being with each mindful breath.

The Sailing Mirror: Reflecting the Authentic Self

Mindfulness, akin to a reflective mirror, becomes the vessel for observing the authentic self. This segment elaborates on how mindfulness practices serve as the mirror's surface. By cultivating self-reflection and self-compassion, readers learn to gaze into the reflective waters of mindfulness, recognizing the beauty and authenticity that reside within.

10.2 Synchronizing Mindfulness with Life's Shifting Tides

Life, an ever-changing sea, demands a synchronization of mindfulness with its shifting tides. This section navigates the art of integrating mindfulness into the ebb and flow of life's transitions. Whether navigating uncharted opportunities, weathering stormy challenges, or navigating the calm seas of routine, readers learn to adapt their mindfulness sails, steering with openness and resilience.

Adapting to Life's Symphony: The Dance of Changing Circumstances

Life's symphony plays diverse tunes, and mindfulness adapts to its changing rhythm. This part is a conductor's guide on integrating mindfulness into life's varied movements. By embracing mindfulness as a companion in both serene and tempestuous seas, readers learn to dance gracefully with life's symphony, tuning in to the present moment's melody.

The Wisdom of Mindful Consistency: Seeds of a Lifelong Practice

Consistency, the anchor of mindfulness practice, is explored as the wisdom guiding a lifelong journey. This subsection uncovers the transformative power held within small, daily moments of mindfulness. Readers gain insight into the significance of regular practice, understanding that the seeds of awareness, when consistently nurtured, blossom into a fulfilling and awakened life.

B. The Depth of Mindfulness: Unveiling Nuanced Techniques

10.1 The Tapestry of Advanced Mindfulness Techniques

Progressing in the mindfulness journey unravels a tapestry of advanced techniques. We dive into the intricate patterns of nuanced mindfulness practices, inviting readers to deepen their understanding and experience. From mindfulness of emotions to advanced concentration techniques, individuals are guided in expanding their practice, weaving threads of sophistication into their mindful tapestry.

The Artistry of Mindfulness Mastery: Painting Nuances with Practice

Mindfulness mastery becomes an art, with each stroke of practice adding nuanced details. This section serves as an artist's palette, illustrating how mindfulness practitioners can paint intricate details into their practice. Through exploration and refinement, readers learn to add depth and richness to their mindfulness canvas, creating a masterpiece of self-awareness.

Immersive Mindfulness: The Symphony of Retreats and Immersions

Mindfulness retreats emerge as immersive experiences enriching the practice's depth. This segment explores the benefits of these retreats, offering guidance on how to incorporate these experiences into a lifelong journey. Through firsthand accounts and practical tips, individuals learn to use retreats as transformative catalysts, diving into the depths of self-discovery.

10.2 Mindfulness: The Conduit to Spiritual Unveiling

In this section, mindfulness becomes the conduit to spiritual exploration and development. We delve into the intersection of mindfulness and spiritual growth, revealing how mindfulness serves as a gateway to a deeper understanding of oneself and existence. Through contemplative practices and philosophical explorations, readers embark on a spiritual journey of profound self-discovery.

Mindful Contemplation: Navigating Spiritual Depths

Contemplation becomes a compass, guiding individuals through the spiritual depths of mindfulness. This part serves as a navigator's guide, illustrating how mindfulness practices open portals to profound self-discovery. By embracing contemplative practices, readers set sail on the vast ocean of spiritual growth, exploring the depths of their existence.

C. The Harmony of Mindfulness in Life's Symphony

10.1 Orchestrating Ambition and Mindfulness

Mindfulness, far from negating ambition, becomes the orchestrator of life's symphony. This section explores the delicate balance between mindfulness and ambition, guiding readers to approach their pursuits with focused intention and a grounded awareness of the present. Mindfulness serves as both conductor and accompanist, harmonizing the pursuit of goals with the contentment of the present moment.

The Composer's Touch: Crafting a Harmonious Life

Life becomes a harmonious composition when crafted with the touch of mindfulness. This part unfolds the metaphor of life as a symphony, with mindfulness as the composer's guiding hand. Through practices that encourage a mindful approach to goals, readers learn to compose a life that resonates with both achievement and contentment.

Relationships as Melodies: The Ever-Changing Harmony

Relationships, akin to melodies, evolve over a lifetime, and mindfulness provides a steady rhythm amidst change. This section explores how mindfulness enriches relationships at different stages—whether in friendships, partnerships, or family dynamics. Readers are guided in fostering enduring connections through the mindful cultivation of compassion, understanding, and presence.

10.2 The Echo of Mindful Relationships Across Lifetimes

Relationships, like echoes across lifetimes, leave a lasting resonance. This subsection reflects on the enduring impact of mindfulness in relationships. Through practices that foster enduring connections, readers learn to sow seeds of intimacy and understanding, creating a symphony of harmonious relationships that echoes across the tapestry of their lives.

Compassion's Melody: Harmonizing Lifelong Connections

The melody of compassion becomes the soulful undertone in lifelong connections. This part becomes a guide to understanding the role of compassion in mindfulness-infused relationships. Through practices that encourage kindness, readers learn to create an ever-expanding orchestra of connections, harmonizing the journey of a lifetime.

10.3 The Legacy of Mindfulness: Footprints in the Sands of Time

As individuals traverse their mindfulness journey, they contribute to a legacy—a legacy of presence, compassion, and awakened living. This chapter concludes with a reflection on the enduring legacy of mindfulness. Readers are invited to consider the impact of their mindful choices not only on their lives but on the world, leaving a positive imprint for future generations.

Footprints in the Sands of Time: Leaving a Mindful Legacy

Mindful living becomes a legacy of footprints in the sands of time. This concluding section serves as a reflection on the enduring impact of mindfulness. Readers are encouraged to recognize the power of their mindful choices, understanding that each step on their journey leaves a positive imprint on the world, inspiring future generations toward a mindful and fulfilling life.

As we turn the final pages of "Awakened Living: Embrace Mindfulness for a Fulfilling Life," I extend my heartfelt appreciation to you, dear reader, for embarking on this transformative journey through the intricate landscapes of mindfulness within the vibrant tapestry of urban life.

From the bustling city streets to the serene corners of self-reflection, we have together explored the profound depths of present-moment awareness. In the ebb and flow of daily life, we've unraveled the interconnected dance of mind and body, unveiling the liberating simplicity found in the embrace of the now.

The chapters within this book have not merely served as guides; they've been invitations to immerse yourself in the practice, to feel the heartbeat of the city pulse with mindfulness. Together, we navigated the complexities of relationships, facing challenges with a mindful resilience that transforms adversity into opportunities for growth.

Our exploration ventured beyond the traditional boundaries of mindfulness, extending into the advanced realms of technique, the immersive experiences of retreats, and the spiritual dimensions that intertwine with our everyday existence. In each step, mindfulness has proven to be a constant companion, adapting and evolving, much like the dynamic city we call home.

As we consider the balance between ambition and mindfulness, nurture relationships through the phases of a lifetime, and reflect on the legacy we leave, let these pages be more than just a book; let them be a compass for your ongoing journey of awakened living.

So, as you close this chapter—both metaphorically and literally—may you carry with you not just the knowledge, but the living essence of mindfulness. May each mindful breath, each intentional action, be a testament to the richness of life when lived with awareness.

This book is not a conclusion; it is a stepping stone. As you navigate the pathways of your life, may the principles of awakened living infuse each moment with purpose, fulfillment, and a deep connection to the beauty that resides in the present.

With immense gratitude and warm wishes for your ongoing journey,

Hristiyan Delev
Author, "Awakened Living: Embrace Mindfulness for a Fulfilling Life"

www.ingramcontent.com/pod-product-compliance
Lightning Source LLC
Chambersburg PA
CBHW080942260726
48661CB00010B/4040